The Oracle Room

FRED JOHNSTON

Published by Cinnamon Press
Meirion House
Glan yr afon
Tanygrisiau
Blaenau Ffestiniog
Gwynedd LL41 3SU
www.cinnamonpress.com

The right of Fred Johnston to be identified as author of this work
has been asserted by him in accordance with the Copyright,
Designs and Patent Act, 1988. © 2007 Fred Johnston

ISBN 978-1-905614-21-9
British Library Cataloguing in Publication Data. A CIP record for
this book can be obtained from the British Library.

Designed and typeset in Palatino by Cinnamon Press
Cover design by Mike Fortune-Wood from original artwork 'look
through a window' © Feng Yu, agency Dreamstime.com

Printed and bound in Great Britain by Biddles Ltd, King's Lynn, Norfolk

Notes and Acknowledgements

On Hearing of the Death of Gerald Davis (p77). Gerald Davis: Dublin-born painter, of Lithuanian Jewish descent, died June 17th, 2005. Played the character of Joyce's Leopold Bloom on many memorable Bloomsday occasions.

An Traonach i bhfolach – The Invisible Corncrake (p.94). A slow air for flute composed by Marcus Hernon, a wonderful player from Carna, Connemara, Co. Galway. The corncrake is all but extinct in Ireland now. Acknowledgements are made to *Studies,* (Dublin) where this poem first appeared as did the poem, *Maps and Sand;* to *The Village* magazine, Dublin, where the poem *Index* first appeared; to *Southword* magazine, the Munster Literature Centre, Cork, for *An Traonach i bhfolach – The Invisible Corncrake;* to *The Arabesques Review,* (Société Arabesque, Chlef, Algérie) for first publication of *At Sousse, Tunisia; The Black Mountain Review,* (N.I.), for *The Suicides; Jacket* 18(Australia) for *The One; The Argotist* (on-line) for *Wrapping;* the editors of *Van Gogh's Ear* (Paris)for *Love is no Defence* and *Mobius* (US) for *The Poet's Lament.*

My thanks to Colin Smythe (UK) publishers, for permission to use lines from 'The Voyage of Snedgus,' from *The Blessed Trinity of Ireland,* by Lady Gregory – Colin Smythe, 1985; lines from 'The Colony Room,' by Medbh McGuckian, by kind permission of Medbh McGuckian and The Gallery Press, Loughcrew, Oldcastle, Co Meath, Ireland, from *Drawing Ballerinas* (2001); lines from *The Shipwreck,* by Michael Hartnett, by kind permission of the Estate of Michael Hartnett and The Gallery Press, Loughcrew, Oldcastle, Co Meath, Ireland, from *O Bruadair* (1985).

There is, alas, no point to try to uncover further works by either the bold Gaius Tuteis, or Jacob Martin Keissler, for neither exists – although I wish I had known them.

My thanks also to the Arts Council of Ireland – *An Chomhairle Ealaíon* – for their generous support in recent years; and to Mr Ulick O'Connor, Esq., writer, poet and literary historian, at *Les Deux Magots,* Paris.

Contents

"… his condemnation of society was wholesale, ranging from hedonism of the rich to the sloth and lawlessness of the lower classes. (He) was convinced that he lived in the worst of times."

'The Ceremonial City: Toulouse Observed, 1738 – 1780.'
Robert A. Schneider:
Princeton University Press, 1995.

The Oracle Room

Love in Those Days

An Indian restaurant was a new thing then,
Before the coming of the condom,
  When sex was being careful.

A plastic Buddha,
Blind and golden in a plastic cave,
  A hiss of sitars from the walls.

Decent mad cafés where
Broke revolution earned a crust –
  Gays held hands under tables.

I was moon-daft in the brick orchards,
Untunable as a Picasso guitar –
  Real girls scoffed at make-up.

You said *Don't call me beautiful*,
Even as a lick of candlelight shaped
  A flawless ikon of your face.

Today's Mystery Voice

Here is today's mystery voice…
I rang, said I knew the voice, knew
When I'd heard it last,
The circumstances, the dark room…
We have to move on, caller…

I asked: How can a man like that
Be on your programme, how can…
I'm sorry, caller…
You don't know who he is, obviously,
You don't understand what he's capable…
I'm sorry, caller, I must insist that you …
I don't understand, I said.
You say he's a famous…
Please don't say anything offensive, caller,

I must remind you you're on air…
You mean on *the* air. What I'm saying is,
That mystery voice of yours
Is no mystery, at least not to me.
And I don't want your money…

Caller, I must be rude and hang up. If
You've nothing more to contribute…
I almost died when I heard that voice,
Now he's famous as a *what*, you say?
Does no one remember the…

That's it, caller, there are other people
On the line, perhaps some other radio show…
Ask him about the stairs, the rooms…
It's a recording, caller…
For Christ's sake, ask him! The windows…
Thank you, caller, and goodbye…

Someone must remember, remember like me,
I can't believe that no one else…
No correct answer today, listeners,
So the prize goes up and we'll
Play our mystery voice tomorrow morning again…

Cobbled

The hotel is run by Algerian Christians,
A postcard Virgin mourns against the cash-register.
In the morning, women move from room
To room, stooping. Breathy falsetto of vacuums.

    No matter where I am, I am always there.
    Rain polishes the regrettable palm,
    There is no one for breakfast. Now is the time
    To make a run for the end of the world,

    To face yourself. *To ignore mirrors.*
    Walk the cobbles of Père Lachaise,
    The morning opens on immaculate tombs.

Night Music

Wind-drunk gulls angle and tip,
A boat lazes like a woman after sex
Stretched on a couch.
It could be anywhere, a time of year
Out of time. The islands ghost away.

Boys pant and sniffle
Waiting for the old men to grunt.
Under the bare arm
Of the diving board, in the dark
That smells of salt.

And in the orange light
Drizzling on the empty promenade,
Snot-nosed other lads brazen out
The smiling cars:
Men of impeccable character fuck them.

Lines Written after a Poetry Festival

Now that the poetry's over
There's Gaza and Iraq,
And the crooked politicians
Doing deals behind our back.

The addicts are still with us,
Single mothers barely twelve:
There's speculators' bagmen
Buying councillors' resolve –

The Yanks still dump their soldiers
In our airports and hotels:
No poet worth a travel-grant
Dare sound the warning bells.

For now the poetry's over
And real life shuts us down,
The old can die on trolleys
As before, without a sound.

The homeless lie in doorways,
The bent and greedy rule –
There's some should be in prison,
But a poet's no-one's fool.

The festival is over,
We're up for sale again –
I'll clam up if the price is right,
You won't hear me complain.

Bomb them back to the stone-age,
It's all the same to us –
The wretched don't read poetry
So what's the bloody fuss?

So what about Geneva,
Conventions and all that?
As a poet I'm unconventional,
So I can wear any hat –

My middle name is Silence,
Now that the boozing's done,
The screwing and back-slapping,
The harmless poetical fun.

The Kafka Prize for Poetry

Maximum of twelve entries.
Visa or Mastercard accepted,
Foreign currency or cheques are not.
Do not send cash.
Poems may be on any theme or subject and in any style,
But be unpublished previously.
All poems must be written in the English language,
The competitor's name must not appear on the manuscript.
The organisers reserve the right to change the panel
Of judges without notice and withhold any or all prizes
If they decide such is justified.
There will be no correspondence.
The submission of an entry implies the unqualified
Acceptance of the rules of entry.
Copyright remains with the author.

Bubble

for Xenia Gerasimova

I will go to Moscow in my head,
See the onion domes peel off their light in the sun,
Walk the Square where, at one side,
Imprecise as a slip of ink on paper
Someone will wave; I will know the sounds
Of the words meshing around me,
The talk of ordinary people making the world:
I will wear a fur hat and wait, as if reading
Towards the end of a story by Lermentov,
For the challenge, the offer of choice of weapons –
While small snow flickers in a change of season
There are boot-prints encrypting in the frozen grass,
When I nod two unmoving figures
                Drown in a welter of spun water.

Warning to the Just-Born

I knew them in their youth
And they sat at the same tables:
Out on the fringes of the world,
The bell of their daily dying rang.
Immeasurably sad, the waste
Of time, good words, possible lives:
Under the same trees new names
Bloom for a time, then blacken
Into the undergrowth we have become.
I would say to the just-born:
Don't come here. Stay away. Find
A warmer, less water-bordered place;
Live at a slow, but always forward pace.

The Poet's House

at Finnavarra, Co. Clare

You enter by walking on water,
The flat miracle of washed stones.
The islands lie like cushions
On the rumpled quilt of the Atlantic –
You can sense a turning in the bones,
At first thrown off like an Autumn shiver
But not quite going. Superstitions
Waddle like swans on the black rock:
You are out of reach of TVs, telephones,
The ordinary others that make you
Sure. The heart gives a consenting quiver,
The outline of the house is visible
Against the hilled wet grasses:
        The scholar-nib's first black incision.

Looking Out

Sitting in a parked car I watch the sea
Age like any man, turn grey as the sun sets,
Tune itself to the tune rehearsed in me,
      And, as I do often, the sea forgets
The peevish rages and the cries and frets
      Which middle-age believes obligatory.

Sea-monsters trawled up dance a galliard
Around the smoulder of a fire lit to illuminate:
An angel-whisper in the heart's unheard,
      There is no guardian biding at the gate
Where angels and monsters might separate –
      I make my choice in the uttered word.

To Winter

You spike anguish into the heart of the year;
    Your handprint is on the left gate-post
    And on the right, the mark of your thumb.

The South path is struck dumb under snowfall,
    The North path is loud with footprints –
    East and West, field and wood are blinded.

You taint the well with parched fingers of ice,
    The poet's bird pecks thirsty verse on verse:
    Familiar roads are dangerous – love frosts over.

Scarier

Scarier than sudden snow
With its cold, virgin blindness
And scarier even than sultry fogs,
Which clog the nostrils with wet
Brown breath from the dead earth –
Scarier than the prick of a thorn-bush
Too far back in the hedge to have
Reached, though it did –
Scarier than thunder or lightning
Or a magpie tumbling off a garden
Wall –
   Scarier than all
   Of these
   Is the sort of thing one sees
Without looking:
A puck-devil grinning on a branch,
A man standing in the middle
Of the midnight road,
Old love in the eyes of the new:
   Scarier this last
   Than the other two.

Balancing Act

You climb a little, leave the road
And the well is there with its watery eye
On invisible mountains over the green rainy
                                        Edge of the North.

One finger tracing the stone's code,
I balance between water, earth and sky
Chanting a name, probably yours, prayerfully
                                        For all I'm worth.

Fantasy

Angling over to swipe
The round Formica with a wiping-cloth,
She frees small breasts the colour
And shape of your chipped cup. Her lips
Move about a small embarrassment.
Table to table, loud men off a building-site
Butter bread, talk with their mouths full.
There is a lull in the day, here between
One o'clock and two; boots whited
With cement, cement flecks in the hair,
They talk of nothing feminine or soft.

She straightens from a table
On which everything is
Doubled: two salt sellers, two sugar bowls,
Two bottles of red sauce.

A young lad, waving an empty glass,
Tries out his being a man. He grunts
At her from a far corner, snuggled there
Among the red round rural faces
And the odour of sweat and scaffold.
He demands something she cannot hear,
Asks for the undecipherable.

The town is full of country boys in corners
Chancing it, finding their measure.
Half the day looking down on wet roofs,
Raised into the air with their own language
And cultural maps,
They demolish and rebuild,
Rough hands roughing up the heart.

At a near table someone else praises
The breasts of a Page Three barmaid from Kent.

Common

There were words I carried in the street,
Phrases tight, ordinary, Elizabethan
That have vanished into Ulster's thin air
Taking their histories with them –
A sort of understanding is erased,
A common tongue, as common as you'd get,
That hedged the bad in with the good
And drew a territory of heart, head, voice
Which, faulted, was our own by birth and choice.

Poetry Class

The self matters. You try to leave
An explanation they'll follow,
That poetry is seeded
In the heart's unreachable space.
But their selves matter; startle here
Their hesitations. To look outwards
Is adventure; inwards
Is too far in the other direction:
No quick returning, no
Unlearning what's revealed back there.
They settle the self into itself again,
A latch let fall, a gate shut.
Tell us what to do next, stubborn voices say:
You are the teacher, show us the way.

The One

He's taken for a novelty now,
But he wasn't always —
Back in the bad days
He ran the place. His word
Was our law. And no harm, either:
The soft welter of him now, you'd
Think he'd never
Been a clever
Man, but he was. He can't sing
Now, but he could, back then.
Only the young can mock like that,
Urging him on
And his voice gone
He's a fool to himself, feeling
The young girls' slim backs
And thinking what was naughty
Forty years ago is naughty now —
I am his son,
I am the one
Who waits while he pisses himself:
I am the one who carries this old Christ
Up the hill to his bed of skulls —
I am the one who rolls the stone over his grave.

Wait

The walls are thick with your absence,
A white sheen of your not being here;
The garden is growing in our separateness,
A pile of ash dries funereally at a corner wall –
When I smile in a shaving mirror,
                    I do not smile, I leer.

I am alone in a muted sort of way,
Waiting for you, snared between times;
All over this city people are drowsing home,
Cyclists shake hysterically, drivers rage and flail –
I hear the off-timing of your black car,
                    As it turns the hill and climbs.

The Bridges

for Nessa O'Mahony

The bridges in new winter light
Dance in their distance and dark.

Weather heaves out of mountain
And deep hysterical sea –

Short days, bitter and sharp,
Street lamps fluttering like lashes:

Coy, too, the unrisen sun
Hand-over-hand up morning's ladder,

Drunk on flagons of night under
The earth: the gardens are out of breath.

Paris from *Le Parmentier*

for Simon Green

This is the centre. You feel
Trains pulse under your feet
Like blood. Here the street
Spokes inwards
               To the hub of a wheel.

The wheel turns. Africa goes
On bare feet, a drum sounds
Or a girl moves like water, drowns
A parched heart,
               And our time slows.

Time slows again. Afternoon,
Flowers blink in flowerpots
Balanced in precarious boxy lots
On high balconies,
               A radio plays a rap-tune.

Rap *francais*; men joke
At the counter over beading beer,
Talk horse racing, hear what they hear
Some argue football,
               A dog sleeps in the smoke.

Letter Before Setting Out

Now that late sun is creeping up the grey wall,
Timid, drying the earlier rain,
I think of you, dear friend, and feel the sweet
Poison of regret that I did not say this or that:
Evening in half-light is a bad time for the heart,
The windows open on empty gardens,
The music on the radio is sad with meaning.
Going away, taking to the air again,
An old bird with loose feathers,
I have left all sorts of things untied and loose.
I'll write – letters take about four days:
Something in people like us
Is always unfaithful to the rest of the world;
                              I will keep on the move.

On the Death of George Harrison, Beatle

November 29th 2001

With you gone, George, we feel our age:
The croppy lads upstairs on the bus, rampant
With new sex, the girls shy-legging it, the air
Full of what we were becoming. Then, we couldn't
Let the flowers grow under out feet, submarining
In this breaking world, neither fish nor fowl.
We wanted to be you, or George Best. Or both.
I finger-strummed a cheap guitar; so did the world.
What I'll miss most is the part of you that's me,
Watching *Help!* in a Belfast cinema, getting
My hair to the length where my father could say
I looked like a *drowndéd rat*. Time enough, then.
    But not now. I watch my hobbling in the
Bathroom mirror, shaving a face too closely-shaved
By every sort of thing. I need more skin, not less.
    Then you're gone, George. Is the music
Enough? You just can't beetle off on me like that;
The gap left's too wide. Into it we all might plunge,
    The flash-Harry wee lads now fat and fifty,
Swinging on your every word.

Satellite

See how the little arrowhead
Wheels soldier-smart on the blue screen
As the taxi turns down a boulevard
Or inserts itself brutally
Between the waxed thighs of cars
Parked too close together –
And how some roads and streets are red
Veins and others colourless:
And the river is always a flat blue,
The Ile de la Cité like a fat slug,
Bridges and streets tying it to the river:
How the point of the arrow
Leaps in quick spasms
That would break you if you really moved that way.

Le Pendu

He dreamed a man hanging
From the roof-beams of the world:
When he left your house
That last time, he must have known:

I will not come back,
I will hang
From the twin horns of the moon.

They're poking under bridges,
Trawling the river; they aren't looking
In the right places. Look up,
At his age, the moon, the sky, is home.

Every window has his image
Postered there, a small face too neat
For the chaos meeting it,
Going public is not what he wanted.

You'll blame yourselves,
He wouldn't want that. He'd say:
I made a grab for the moon,
I got hooked on it, that's all.

At the *Hotel de Ville*

for Marcia Lebre – July 2003

They are chanting
Beneath red banners,
Young Paris girls partying, the CRS
Black on the black street,
Shoulder-pads, batons, transparent shields,
Chadors of iron wrap
Round the sneers of the armoured vans –
They advance,
Obey their stage-directions and fall back.
Under a lamp-post poster of Marlene Dietrich,
A simmering light trickles
Like electricity on the rims of the riot-shields.
A sudden run, the noise
Voices make blowing over pavements:
In the painted face of the Hotel de Ville,
TV cameras arc their booms
Like irritating flies; a girl on a bicycle smiles
Past, her skirt rises,
The bored black knights chewing gum
Pull down their visors –
A young man on skates pirhouettes
Just to see what's going on,
A tourist takes quick photos,
A father holds an infant up to the barrier's
Edge, taxis slam under the tunnels –
This is how the world will begin and end.

Crossing

on hearing of a death

Then you cross the border and news comes
Down hard like a stamp on a passport –
There is a mark on you visible only to the heart.

Yesterday, a matter of hours, the road was clear
And there were trees whistling in the wind
Of your coming and going, hedges bowing, light.

Now the bags are heavier and you look for help
To find a familiar hotel, everyone drives
On the wrong side of the road, it's a new language.

It's not fun, you wait in the sand, no-one comes:
The guidebook says you should be there, but
You're here, sagging under a sky bright as bone.

Weather Vane

The brightening hedge,
Tendril ache in the tree,
Yellow fevered flower,
Lap of stale water in the gutters –

The tourists come, bulbous
With backpacks, tuberous with
Cameras, shuttering
In streets of empty salt wind –

Let us praise the ever-leafing plane,
The reach upwards to the new,
The piratical B&B, the fat shamrock,
The evergreen sun, the weather-vane.

Rendition

In a London B&B you bend to fix your shoe
And your spine cracks, splits, something slips,

Then you're a cripple, crying out in pain
And no doubt our neighbours think it's sex

But you're trundled in a wheelchair across
Heathrow tarmac, doped with over-the-counter

Painkillers, permitted to be the first to board,
Your face – which has leaned over me so often

In the night, scrutinising my own for a flicker
Of light, a sign that I am some sort of loving man –

Frowns and breaks as we gather speed and twitch
Into the concrete sky, you seated painfully apart:

As if under orders the cabin crew watched us both,
Attentive, careful, as if we might do something stupid.

Index

The last letter my daughter sent spelt it out:
I am going to manage international finances, do

With numbers what you say you do with words,
Mix them, rearrange them, maybe even make

Them make sense, who knows? Anyway, I have
No interest in music or poetry. Nor in you.

Each time a FTSE or a Dow quote scampers like
A white rat across the bottom of the TV screen

I wonder if that's her, tucked up in the land of
Cuckoo clocks and chocolates, making the numbers

Jump. I think of a book of my poems I sent her
Years ago, how those words remain the same,

Aren't traded up or down; I'd love to have a line
Of one of those poems slide over the screen, see

If a plus or minus sign appeared suddenly
After it, know that she's out there, quoting me.

The Nothing Wrong

You could come out of there if you wanted to:
A piano plinks out across a yard and a dog yaps,
There's a crack in the gate where lightning
Savaged the concrete, the fields are wet –

Still your half-door's open on the lilt of Chopin,
You're thin as a man consumed –
The old dog's there quavering the still air
Where no one comes, and the rooms are dark –

This is a place of boggy green, of no laughter,
Of roads where dust settled, stayed, of walks
Alone in the evening with a fettering ache
In the gut; though doctors say there's nothing wrong.

The Sound of Please

for Orhan Pamuk

Possibility is everything –
It's the essence, some say.
She could have been everything

That is possible but changed
Into a tired woman leaning
Against a file-cupboard, changed

Only by the urgency of computer
Screens pinging irrelevancies,
Letters untyped, a computer

Whose printer's jammed. This
Is the name and count
Of what she's become, this

Is, somehow, not right –
All that vitality scrapped into
A dustbinful of paperclips, right

Beside the same desk and chair,
And a window on the carpark,
A calendar hanging over the chair

With red circles marking off
Those peevish days of blood
And longing; the phone's off

Its cradle, she will not answer
The same questions over
And over, there is no answer

To why she still inhabits this
Place, a room of artificial light,
When she could leave all of this

And go. There is a world
To argue with, to oppose,
Outside this grey-walled world

But her breath goes when
She imagines a door opening –
She loses her breath when…

Let's

Let's make off into the world, the two of us
Telling no one we're going –
Let's book the flight, take the bus
Go without them knowing.

It's coming winter with the garden chaotic
And every window shut tight –
There is no air passing through the house
Each morning falls straight into night.

So let's make a run for it under cover of cold
And leaf-fall, of scouring sea-rain –
Before they try to stop us, the well-meaning
Impossible friends, and make us explain.

The Poet's Lament

after the 19th cent. Breton gwerz 'Mallor ar Barz koz O Vervel'

After a hundred years
there is neither seeing nor hearing;
And so I curse my ageing.

Having spoken for a hundred winters
my tongue is frozen;
So I curse the winter.

Having laughed for a hundred winters,
my tears are frozen;
So I curse sorrow.

Having had speed in my sinews and strength,
I am myself frozen:
I curse all things that move.

Having wept at the dying of friends,
I have no friends left;
I curse my friends.

Having touched beautiful women,
my fingers are numb;
I curse beauty.

Having had so long a life,
I am caged up in my own bones –
And so I curse life.

Learning French Slang

Tonight we will learn
Gonzasse, mec, salaud
And even flirt with *pute.*
There are other words, a question
Of degree, *minable,* for instance,
And gestures never to be made,
With two fingers or crossed arms.

I will nurse these words and signs
Little nuts of bitterness, until
They root on my tongue,
Graft themselves to muscle and bone.

Dance Night in the Village

Last night I saw them
As if they hadn't been there before:
The dancers dancing a dream of a new place,
Middle-aged women on stools at the bar,
While two fiddlers, a bloke with a guitar,
(a Londoner, sixty if a day)
Played jigs and reels –
They'd come to this Irish village
With only the sea to contradict them
Looking for the man or boy who'd tricked them
A handful of decades ago,
And they'd hold on to him when they found him.

Why do they come,
What do the rocks and feral goats
And winds wet as weekend washing offer them?
It's a sad cabaret, all this, the notion of exile
As salvation, as if you can crawl out of one skin
Into another just like that –
Old local men ignore them, mutter about
The new houses going up on the pastures
And good acres. One Manchester man boasts
He's had a woman twice his age; did he have
To come to the edge of Ireland to manage that?

Last night I saw
How I fitted in to all of this,
How I should take you and get out
Before it seems attractive.
In bed, we consulted maps of France –
You won't find us dancing that old dance.

Maps and Sand

for El Hedi El Abed, painter
  El Kantaoui, Tunisia - May, 2004

We name ourselves in sand:
Characters like blown thin grass in a sea breeze
Among the angled needles of fishing-rods
And the bloom of umbrellas –
A sky as endless as we think it is,
Balconies that blind under the noon sun.

At Sousse, Tunisia

Downhill by rust-dead railway tracks
To the seafront, salt breeze, a patient line
Of horse carriages stiff as postcards,
Past leather bag shops, the lovely gaggling
Girls, old women wrapped head to toe
In butter-coloured cloth, a man posing without
Meaning to at an angle to an ancient streetlamp –
A sailor's spit from Carthage and its tomb
         This always-exile once again goes home.

Blind Music

All week and more a sheet of cloud
Glaucomic and cold
Has hung over the garden and the town:
In my perch by the hearth
I have no words for you. I am silent
As old men go quiet in the head,
Unresponsive as the garden's
Grey brick wall. No matter how you
Try, you cannot rouse me,
The young-enough man you met,
Who has put on this indifferent skin
And raises his voice only to complain.

Imagining younger men looking
At you, I tell myself
It is no more than your due. Have fun.
Get out of the blind house,
It's eyelash of cloud. Find sweat
And heat, a trickle of fire in the gut.
But come back. I will say nothing.
I will remain as I am,
Unaltered even by a flicker of envy –
What I do not tell you
Is that, even under this bleached dead
Sky I have a tune in my head:

A chant of guilt, perhaps,
But a tune nonetheless,
With no words to go with it. Not yet.

Morning in the Burning House of Mirrors

Ou d'avoir été blessé le souvenir la brulera devant moi... "
                              - Christian Guez Ricord (1948-1988)

He woke up to the smell of burning,
Startled himself
In the armchair,
Danced on the dark stars flowering on the carpet:
Later, he awoke to the smell of longing,
Which is a kind of burning.

How to say to her, angled in the sun-cold
Morning window,
That no amount
Of polishing would erase the bruise forming
On his heart, bleeding outwards
And staining them both –

He was not skilled at putting out
Small fires:
He did not have her discipline,
And the odour of burned wool lay over
The room in spite of everything –
His face surrounded him, she had
          Polished up an avalanche of mirrors.

Conversation on a Staircase

Do you know the story of those Breton
Women, called witches, who,
Because they had cured an ailing cow or
Tamped down a child's fever,
Found themselves harassed into the forests
And there, hunted,
Huddled themselves in doe-skins to keep
The shape of a woman from men's eyes?

What skin will you put on
To stop me seeing you as you really are:
Prancing about the room, hiding
                    In a thicket of words?

The Bed

It must be like this to wake up
On a bed from which the view is not home
But some other-where attained by chance
And the lover dressing now at the window
Is poised with one leg raised on a chair
The bow of her spine taut in a Degas bend
And one fragile white breast visible –
There is a train you can hear distancing
Itself from the town whose red roofs
Are thuds of paint in a blue sky,
An accordion tune the girl hums,
Behind the papered walls, workmen
Arguing and laughing –
    But I am on my own bed and
The street in the window is my own:
It is not the woman dressing who is strange
But the figure filling my own skin,
Whose body is carved from new anxiety,
Shaped like an exclamation mark,
    Waiting for words to catch up.

The Suicides

The suicides come empty-faced out of the sea
Netted with weeds and wrack and grass
Thrown on the rocks of the year's end, usually
In the witless dark, under mad Christmas lights.
Some travel farther in the out-dragging tides
Than they ever did when they could laugh –
As if distance was the real terror, and they knew:
The water turns their eyes the colour of pearl,
The colour of the moon in winter, or winter fog.
Others hold close in to the old landscape,
Close a door, inspect the sky-maps on the ceiling,
Leap and never land, which was always the wish:
We who tidy up, sluice away memory's confetti,
Shake the last, last hand, are recast in the stone
Image of the dead. Their miraculous grainy light.

There is No Need

"There are no certain conclusions to be reached regarding the mathematical probability of everyone, sooner or later, finding an island within themselves, which welcomes them."
                              - *Jacob Martin Keissler:* 'Numbers and Knowledge'

To go into the front room where the dead man
Lies, guarded by a candle and a neighbour –
Out on the dead black rocks under a growling sea.

To ask the question in the island's only shop
Why everything's pricier than on the mainland, and
You're mistaken for another woman with the same name:

To ask why we're here, like something breeze-whipped,
Hanging back into ourselves, collecting the pieces, yet
Not having a shape or memory of what we ever were or are.

To wonder why we give our children names in Irish,
Making sounds of them to go out into the world, like bits
Of language on bare feet scattering in search of a rhyme –

To bother with the woman in the Post Office,
Who has a question balanced on her lips for you, and
Will one day tip it out into the air from behind her wire veil.

To be angry at the drunken young man who has never
Seen anything like you and who can't see you now, who
Forgets he abuses you in Irish, words of love gone haywire.

To look behind you in the dark up the hill and back to
The mainland where a vigil at a dead man's bed, once seen,
Was gaffed in the mind like an algebraic riddle: *If $x + y = a + b$...*

Midsummer, Low Tide

"And by order of God a clerk came to
them out of the island to relieve them, for they
were in a bad way for the want of food . . . ."
                              - Lady Gregory: *The Voyage of Snedgus*

They said they'd waited but the tide
Was now too low for the boat to come.
Yawning in a salty heat they'd eyed
Through a pub window a brassy bay
Then left it, coming late to the house
Where we'd eaten before them, slopped
White and red wine, while their places
Set without them looked in mourning –
Music had been arranged and some sort
Of celebration for the boat's arriving:

Black swells of cloud pushed out of the sea
And pissed like drunks without apology
On the cooling windows and the shrubbery.

Tomorrow will be better and the boat
Will lollop in; they'll go down
Again to photograph her crew,
Kiss the captain who'd circled the globe
As if he'd rescued them: TV cables
Will eel in the trimmed grass,
There'll be cakes, handshakes, a plaque
To mark the hour, the day, he came in:
It will be a sort of birthday on the quay.

But not today, the tide is low -
Killing as grief, they'd had to up and go
From a wet pub table to a micro-waved dinner
Among people they already know.

Wrapping

"For instance, Siculus Pontius was afraid to appear in public unless wrapped, virtually head to foot, in his thickest toga. Yet if he were trying to hide, he had made himself the most stared-upon figure in Rome...."

- Gaius Tuteis: 'On Explanation, bk.IV'

The wind is like a second skin wrapping
The postman sheltering at our door,
And we won't open it, amazed at the way
His body is shaped by his coat, his face
Sparkling with bleeds of rain, and the gasp
On his lips, a plea, not to be left to drown
Or breathe his last while two faces stare at him
Through the thin glass
                    As if he were no longer human.

At Tullyish Churchyard

for George Martin

He's beside you from nowhere:
That church is where Yeats' grandfather
Was rector, there's a plaque inside the door.
Up a lane to the broken tower,
We can always call at the rector's house
For a key. He'll not mind.
       You get this here, a blunder
       That takes all in, matches
       Like for like, insists.
       Take a photograph, wave
From the car door pulled against
A sharp swipe of bitter leafy cold –
       He's given you something to think about.

X-File

"If you are touching, you are also being touched...."
                    - Medbh McGuckian: *The Colony Room.*

In a Dublin restaurant,
Self-service, hot light,
A bald man like any other
Said he fixed small countries.

He said this like you would
Say: *I work in a garage* –
That was what he did,
In his grey raincoat he looked

Like a businessman
Caught between flights,
His accent polite Mid-West
Campus American.

He was hungry, we both
Were: comparing the prices
Of café breakfasts here
And in Belfast, started it.

He knew that city,
He mentioned a good hotel;
Balancing a full tray while
Holding a briefcase isn't easy.

*Do you think we need
Fixing?* I said. *You'd know better
Than me,* he answered,
Knifing up two squares of butter.

Grey

for Dette McLaughlin

Is the sky off the Atlantic, is
                  A child's body in rubble

Is the wall around my garden, is
                  The colour of silence

Is the colour of ash,
                  The flesh of forgetting.

Sitters

Dark evenings sit them down,
One each side of the fire.
There's a low flat sighing of the town
Going about its coming home.

He wishes she'd want him again
She feels much the same:
They open small mouths to explain
But only cigarette smoke comes out.

Years pass like empty trains,
In the beginning, there was sound:
A smouldering quiet reigns,
Mops up their scalded language.

A coal catches, a blue feather
Tickles a tissue of soot –
There's always hope of weather
Changing, or a cup of tea.

Three Elements of Continuity

I

naked branches scalded frost-white
wheel-drift on a roll of black ice
breath in the air the colour of exhaust smoke.

II

your betrayal when it came in an envelope
its weight of paper pleasing to hold and snug
as a balanced gun loaded with shapely bullets.

III

a tension between six o'clock and midnight
when the carpet of ourselves lies under our feet
marks of trampling scouring the elegant patterns.

Examination

under the microscope
of mind, scalpel of imagination
a leaf, branch, bird, bridge becomes
greater than a handful of galaxies.

> to look so closely
> at anything
> is to diminish the looker.

as you inspect my face
as the door closes behind you,
you become smaller. The sum of all
the unimportant decisions of a day,

> the nothings that matter:
> how is it explained,
> your light travelling this far?

The Oracle Room

a room above a river:
>trees in the window,
>veins stripped of skin –
>everything coldly obvious

odour of old incense:
>as if a ceremony
>or consecration
>had taken place.

in this room I'd wait,
>still hungry for words:
>sometimes the phone
>would ring on the bare desk.

Between Waking and Sleeping

in my dream you had died
and
between waking and sleeping,
when light entered the room,
you would not answer my touch:

> in the brittle February afternoon,
> light on the garden so fragile
> it was like water drying up on a green rock,
> you said: You were shaking me.

in my dream you had died. I answered,
still half asleep, *I thought you were dead.*

Hanged Man

the hanged man becomes a cartoon
      his executioner looks embarrassed –

the company board fidget with the report
      stupefied by their own insolence –

anything human is flawed: laws
      imply a given perfection –

walking for the last time to his car –
      or, for the first time, to his execution,
      the executive and the murderer
      suffer for what we fail to be.

Landfall

for Geraldine O'Reilly, painter

coming in from the island, the boat used to you,
it's not like coming home, more
a necessity of living close to the edge of things,
blurred, paintable horizons seen
from a thumb of rock: here the harbour's foul
with oil and diesel, and old friends get you down –
shop now, as a child might sleep, ease away
from what bad news they chant in your ear;
shed their griping the way burnt skin heals:
paint the sun boiling in the saucepan of the sea,
take the boat again when you need what you need.

Pathology

an old friend who wrestled the world as you did
dies of cancer
the catch in your own throat a harmless twinning
brought on by surprise –
there were others, the suicides
and the dead
marriages, trysts meant to outlive life, heart-mined,
or splittable as mercury –
now that mole on your arm spikes like a star,
the pump stops and will not start,
no matter how you cough –
you have their names in your head like aneurysms
on the brink of blowing,
sudden, pain-bright, and when it's over, nothing.

Small Town Music

The lead violinist
Of the Ballymacuseless
Quartet stomped his
Feet in the corner pub
And stated with force
That the town would
Only have a Music School
If he were made its Director,
And certainly not otherwise.

This knowledge was common
As himself. Yet the local
Newspaper ignored it,
No reporter made a single
Telephone call. He was
A highly respected man,
A community stalwart,
And the editor went to school
With his big brother.

So, we are the village
With no music but his:
Ballymacspineless,
We scourge each other,
*Drag him into the new
Century.* And it dawns on us
Only very late in the day
That *he* is the new century,
As they say: *in tune with reality.*

Sex Ring Vanishes Shock!

As every national
Newspaper printed the trades,
Professions, occupations of the dozen
Members of the town's rent-boy
Sex-ring,
Police investigating
The case announced
That there would be no prosecutions
And the matter was, basically, closed.

A bloke who ran his own community
News sheet made newsy inquiries,
Was visited late at night by members
Of a special police unit he had
Hitherto
Believed investigated
Only crimes against
The State.
This is a true story. It is
Up to you whether you believe it.

The town is no different from yours:
It has trap doors and fail-safe mechanisms,
And holes were nosey people
Trip and fall. You do what you must.

Inkscratch

for John Moriarty

One day more desolate than the rest
He climbed into the mountains and felt
The child-hug of stone upon stone.

The stone is warm under the rain,
The roads of the hurried world are
A long way below, varicose, narrowing.

And how to describe a lake, grey
As sky, light as air, an absence in fields
Of gorse, a blow to the cheek, whitening?

The scribes are in their cradle-huts
Plotting the end of poetry. The heron is
Patient. If words come to him here, he'll

Borrow them and speak them to a small
Room. There is a soft line of track
Punctuated by droppings, a paragraph

Beginning itself in sheep-bleat
Higher up, a page turning in heather-lick:
There the sun, drying the inkscratch of his days.

Single Notes

Single notes played on a piano,
One after the other like a child learning to walk
And from somewhere else radio talk,
The red drip of a flower whose name we've mislaid
Slumped against the garden wall,
A wet swipe of sun going down, fade
To winter and its cold poetics,
Adjusted clocks, clicks
And tweaks in wallpipes, letters for debts unpaid –
Summer washes her hands of us, gouts of rain
Pound on cracking frosts,
All imagined enemies take on form, insane
Beliefs are creeds, sleepless we tally costs
And gains of fretful words heartfelt, said
On hot afternoons down a too-available telephone
When heat and long clear evenings left us lonely
And, what's worse, alone –
Winter does the worst or best remembering,
Brown thoughts like old photographs with edges curled
Fall upwards from their safe cupboards in the heart, settling
On the frozen bone
Of the skull, a gallery of peevish sins
                         Against a very personal world.

Killaloe

for Carlo Gebler

A white mist curves round the mountains
Like a fur stole on an elegant woman's neck,

The river is a mirror, the sky shaves in it,
A lather of cloud flicks onto the bone fields.

On the bank a church, black in shadow,
Waits for boats up the river, men in plunder-hurry

Who'll rage-leap the walls and blatter the gate
With an axe. A scarf of smoke drifts on its face.

Now-and-then gathers in pools round the stone
Legs of the bridge, memory is a current against

A current. The streets labour upwards into silence,
Light yellow as the wrapper on a Cadbury's Flake.

An Dro

Dark and cold in Josselin,
The English Bookshop shuttered:
The castle bled into the river –
La-la-lalala-lo!

Up a cobbled hill, wet with fog,
A café, light sugary and warm,
A family affair, closing up –
La-la-lalala-lo!

Je suis un rat de Josselin
Je fait le trou sous les rues –
J'étais le pilleur des poubelles:
La-la-lalala-lo!

There's a song here of a son
Running among the she-deer,
And of a beautiful girl at Mogoar –
La-la-lalala-lo!

On Hearing of the Death of Gerald Davis

Saturday, June 18th, 2005

Any other Bloomsday you'd up and bloom,
Leopolding, immaculate Poldy: not this time.

Two days ago your Dublin lost its bowler hat,
Went bare-headed to your not-being-there.

Two small paintings creep up my wall,
A Mask, a Window, twin elements, camouflage,

A world framed: you said I knew your art,
Which was more compliment than I deserved.

I went away from every meeting with a Jazz
CD like a bright, surreal coin in my pocket –

That last gush, blast, *Yes Yes Yes* of work
Seared the eye, went beyond itself, must have

Left a gash in you, the best you'd done; a
CD spinning now, like a model of the universe,

Fogs my cold sitting-room with *Kaddisch,*
A held top note on the last word, a flourish,

A defining brush-stroke, wing-lift of an ending:
You'd layered so much colour on all that silence,

Voicing each painting, participles of style,
A Capel Street of contrast, a Grafton Street

Of shade, tone, a kidney-breakfast of composition,
A riddling Sandymount of the imagination; still

From wall to wall this labyrinth of self-shaping
Ran indecipherable yet obvious, a willing

Into the face of a sheet blank as death of
Mythographic, musical, bullish, last images,

A plump cave-painter busy in the half-light
Of a skittishly pagan Plurabella moon –

No escape this time on self-impaling wings,
Feather-tips curled inwards in a tabernacular heat -

You heard the wax melt, saw bright drops
Fuse in Howthy sand, felt the laughing descent into light.

Protest

Under the watchdog eye of the police
They made a fire, clapped, protested:

Piled in the rough tent were boxes
Of biscuits, bread, milk: they sang Lennon,

Dylan, and dull men in a silver car
Photographed them. In the dulling sky

Aircraft angled upwards and down,
It grew colder, then very cold, the fire

Snapped and drew back. Beyond
A perimeter fence warplanes dozed.

He had never known her in full
Flight of the things she took to heart,

Her bones touchable even through
A thick coat, a bird-girl, hopping from

One argument to the next – while
He, scanned by the fire of her, became

More see-through by the second,
A refugee in his own heart: they smoked,

Tired, stoked the blackening branches,
He waited for her to wage love, not war.

Love is No Defence

for Michel Houellebecq

Let's be aware that we are not as free
As we like to think,
That there are birds in our heads bearing
Messages to a watching world.

Love is no defence:
We stare into each other's eyes
In the mischievous dark, smoking,
And the tips of our cigarettes

Are signals to the enemy, red
Flares. Similarly,
A willingness to speak out
Is not usable in court: many condemn

Themselves through enthusiasm,
Or bravery. We must be whores,
Like the others. Then no one will mark
Us from a distance, we may even prosper.

Often – as a symptom of what is
To come – we will hear the doorbell
Ring, but when we look, there's no one
Outside. Perhaps a car pulling away, that's all.

Bombs in London

July 7th, 2005

Soho: a rank of doors
Like stale mouths open
On tasteless sex –
The Abbey had been a shout
In stone,
Loud as the whisping tyres
Of bicycles,
Thin cargoes of men in bowlers
Lisping by –
I had walked in sunlight
Light and omelette-yellow,
Lunched civilly in a gallery,
Read with bleak curiosity
phone-box ads for carnival whores.

Gone now,
That postcard London in my head,

Shredded by a knife-
Sharp photo
Of a woman's face clowned
In a medical turban,
Black eyes
Blood-panicked:
A bus decapitated
Yellow stalks bent where
Seats had been,
A gouty red garden
Plant accidentally mowed –

Arriving now
Like a late train, the dead news

In its wrap and warp –
Siren-whine and sound-bite,
Pixels falter on the TV screen
So that every moving image
Spasms forward, reluctant,
                    painfully slowed.

Treason

Lifting his eyes to the cold bright garden
He feels it harder every time to look
Out on the walled privacy he never visits,
Walled as a book.

He stands up in front of them each week
In the blinky gleam of strip-lighting,
He gives them rules he cannot obey
And is tired of fighting.

How to write poetry, or publishable prose:
He has a duty to tell the truth
But he has told it before, it's blunt
As an old man's tooth.

He does not say there were alternatives,
The story of his middle years
Begins and ends with choices
Smudged by fears.

He's moved beyond regret to teaching
A dozen of them twice a season –
Lies of metaphor, tricks of grammar
Poetry as treason.

The Same

for P.D.

It would have been the same
When, turning to Punk and Goth for meaning,
You saw the tide framed over and over
In the panelled window, the harbour
Bored rotten with boats –

Blue gun-metal slates of a village
Dawdling its way up a hill, becoming invisible
Under a sea bright as mercury:
Behind the pub rats tinkered
Among the empty barrels –

The sky would have worn itself out
Trying to move on; doors always creaked.
There would have been a framed poster
Of a dead agricultural fair
Playing mirror to your small face:
                    It's still hanging there,
                    Everything's in its place.

Man Alone Among Headstones

I am a man alone among headstones, searching
Each one,
As if peering, lost, into the faces of strangers.

But these are dangerous times, and a mother,
Watering grave-flowers,
Warns her infant daughter: *Do not go off on your*

Own, do not wander away like that. Water trickles
Like a child's laugh
Into a green plastic bucket. I am a man alone among

Headstones, and that single rose wrapped in its
Cellophane
Could be a ruse, a disguise, my puzzlement an act.

I cannot find you – so often, we couldn't find
Each other,
And the feeling was like this, a child lost, anxious –

And when I do, that skittish joy, a sense of every-
Thing making sense:
The gold lettering of the stone's last line limps down

At an angle. Who could have been so careless not
To know that
I would come, with the invisible others, and we'd see?

I bed the flower between two pots, fearing
The God-scouring
Atlantic wind. I settle the rustly head. I drizzle cold

Water over it and on the neat dry earth. Here
We do not argue,
We do not fight, you are always on time, I am quiet

And, for once, I listen. I hear far traffic and tree breeze,
The pebbly crack
Of mother and child leaving by the path. Nothing else.

In a Hospital

Make out the busy green trees in a distance of yellow roofs,
Turn up a driveway out of the city into rich green air,
Where tubercular patients waited out the months, or a year:
Scaffolding rubs its veins of rust against salt-stripped
Walls, there is the predictable disorientation, a need for maps
Then corridors over-warm, the sun annihilates the grass
Beyond the wide windows: old convalescent balconies open
Only to staff, there is the sea in the distance, teasing as good
News; everyone must wash his, or her, hands, door-handles wait
In ambush, there is *No Smoking*; you can see a young man's leg
In a mediaeval grip of iron and screws, he is trying to sleep,
An arm across his eyes like a man blinded or shot,
There is, viewed through a half-open door, the unimaginable
Loneliness of an old man from the islands, his English is not good,
The few words he has he shouts to make himself hear himself, it
Is unbearable, looking at him: the nurses young, irreconcilably
Pretty, concerned; how they do this work a wonder and
Something we talk about when, leaving you on clean sheets
Waiting in your own desolation more painful than the pain be-
Cause it infects all of us, knowing a doctor will
Explain everything and we are loving and impatient: we go,
Bright hot sunshine rakes our skin, we smell hard dry grass,
Driving, the inside of the car breathless, and we turn
On the radio to let other voices in, drip-feed of riot, murder,
Weather, until we are dulled and ready for this familiar world.

Rogue

In the half-Irish called English here
The word outstretches itself:
Admiration's in there, forgiveness also,
And the moral adultery of envy –
So that when this long, bony man dumbly
Tosses his hands over a young girl
Like a tree folding branches over a grave,
Her face grotesque with embarrassment –
And fear, let's not forget fear – in the
Pub-thawed street at midnight, hungry
As a cow not fed, mewing in his throat,
We look on, slap our shoulders, say
He's the awful rogue, and excuse him his
Playful rape, we are telling the girl, as
She twists away, smiles, sad and sick,
She can expect no sympathy here, not
Where *a rogue* is concerned – and say
Nothing of what we've heard of his wife's
Broken silences and the eyes of the house
Blind too, the rooms deaf; he was hard
Against that girl in the street, an old man
Still rampant, ugly; an image in her head,
A grinning wreck of a grandfatherly farmer
His hands, his crotch, stiff with the smell of dung.

The Beauty Barn

"…but after all that, here in old shoes I stand –"
    – Dáibhí O Bruadair: *The Shipwreck*, trans. Michael Hartnett.

…is a space large enough
to hold sky and earth and sea,
and yet have no room for me

though yesterday I was at the
gate glaze-eyed with their young
men's gazing, my fingers stroking

the inside of my thigh, a heart
big as a bucket, full, blood-sore,
a horse-roar in my ears, a tideful

of salt water and sea-smell
between my legs, a crease of the
gate pushing my arms like a man…

but it was in my head, and stayed
there, a purple feeling; I shook
hot wind out of my hair; loosened,

it blew every which-way; I threw off
stockings, went in bare legs, gave up
make-up or the wish for a new blouse:

hid in a man's loft out of the weather,
and he cut me a window through
the dried flat thatch, gave me a world

a couple of feet square: from there
I could see the street like a blue tongue
teasing the lips of the harbour: my heart

was a belly an hour after sour eating,
stretched, empty, needing to be filled again –
a heart a barn's size, a cathedral of fleshy vein

with a bird twitching in the beams
for good measure, a fingernail of feather
drawn over the pulse of it, repeating, repeating...

Saint Ursula and the Birds

This street turns in on itself
Like a child scolded;
A car wheel's clamped in an iron sound,
It's all muscle and go,
Neon lettering falls out of its adjective
Over windows drizzled with dirt –
Something before our time was maimed and hurt.

Between the hungry hedges
She bends and rises,
Scutting this and ferreting that,
Tamping outrageous energy
Back to its rightful place.
A bird-house dangles like a toy in a crib,
Or a single drop of coloured ink from a nib.

It's a scraggled garden
With a woman light as a leaf
Working it in a wet stillness:
It's not worth the bother
We say, who cannot stand the worry
Of grass under our feet –
Only sure of ourselves, truly complete

On harder surfaces:
She has a story of how the young
Chant madly for their mother,
How the seasons bring them –
Story done, she trowels it
Into the grey, deaf, senseless loam:
She'll dig here all the summer days to come.

To a Friend Sour'd as a Poet

If yet we laugh'd at nicest things
'twas long time since, and Fame hath devill'd
at the task of Poet –
All men who knew thee know it
To be truth,
You are a lesser man who now such poesy sings
Have grown unmannerly, *hélas!* uncouth.

Raiséd red on high a glass to toast
Your new found call, manikins gay livery'd
Garland your breath'd air –
The ugly-soul'd, the virgin fair
Bow from the knee –
God maketh Heaven, but by your ownèd boast
Hath not a portion that proportions thee.

Luminosity

"La femme de ménage est belle comme un don du ciel..."
                    - Jean-Claude Martin: *Raison Garder*

for Kristian le Bras

The luminosity of her small face is what took his eye,
There was no other word for it, a fleshy brightness blinking
In vacuous, unsentimental heat, and the church door where the
Paris Communist shot the Kommandant of the city – he being
A well-liked and cultured man, his death was a moral shock, as
Much as the executions afterwards were, let's say, a physical one,
Was weathered like a face too many years smiling into the rain,
The streets fell down towards the tram lines and the canals
Varicose as old limbs, varicoloured with children, stalls, a plaster of
sun, young men standing seriously at newspaper kiosks, Proud girls
waiting for them forever in the windows of shops,
The bronchial stutter of a motorcycle over the snide backbite of a dog:
Every table had an ashtray and we smoked in the hot wind
Watching her skip like an intrusion of virtue between the iron legs,
Newspapers opened at pages of torture, mutilation, child-rape;
A slump on the Bourse or as indicated elsewhere by Dow Jones,
A TV clattering about nothing over a shaded brown bar
Stacked with lottery tickets, men in checked shirts
Stowing themselves away – Light is personal,
To each eye a different quality of shade, colour,
No more to be shared than any other intimacy.
But undeniably she was gifted in the eyes and mouth.
His word for this was –
                    luminosity.

Wall, Plaque, Book

for Milan Richter, poet

a plaque on the schoolyard wall says
soldiers came here twice (not once, but twice)
the teachers and the schoolchildren left with them,
there were trains snuffling at Drancy
like old men with bad colds –
a separation like a great wound opening.
I do not have to be told that this was horror
beyond horror, that God created such events
to prove to us the existence of Hell –
no more walls, then, no more wire,
ditches and wrecked houses, no more absences:

God's music abhors an interval –
He consults his Book of the Damned
for a scream loud enough to kill the scalding silence.

An Traonach i Bhfolach

for Marcus Hernon

The mad corncrake is no longer in the fields,
Big machines have cut him away.

He is harvested out of his home,
Is there anyone who has heard him lately?

The odd places he scatters to these days,
He keeps quiet and out of our sight.

There is something lonely in the thought
Of his silence: I will be silent like him, but

Not as much lamented. I will be harvested.
My cropped field will throw up a new

Thing, not in the least like me:
If you have a tune for me, now's the time for it.

Birdsong

i.m. Micheal Hartnett, file

The small bird
For the high branch
And the sweetest song.

Opening Windows

In the opening of windows
The house is filled with light:
Sudden as the switching on
Of a new sun impossibly bright,
The rooms recoil, sway, hold,
The hallway is a cavern
Of yellow illumination and black
Shade. The garden
Burns like a dish of mercury:
Out of the trees a bird
I have not seen before, dancing –

It was just before midday I heard
The sound of the miraculous
Break like a wave over the ordinary.